THE SHIRE COOKBOOK

by Chelsea Monroe-Cassel

The Shire Cookbook

This cookbook is a fictional work loosely inspired by the works of J.R.R.Tolkien. It is in no way authorized or approved by the Tolkien estate, his heirs, or Middle-Earth Enterprises. It is intended to honor the legacy of a great man who taught so many of us to both dream of adventure and to value a sense of home.

Find more information at:
www.TheShireCookbook.com

ISBN-13: 978-0692472255
ISBN-10: 0692472258

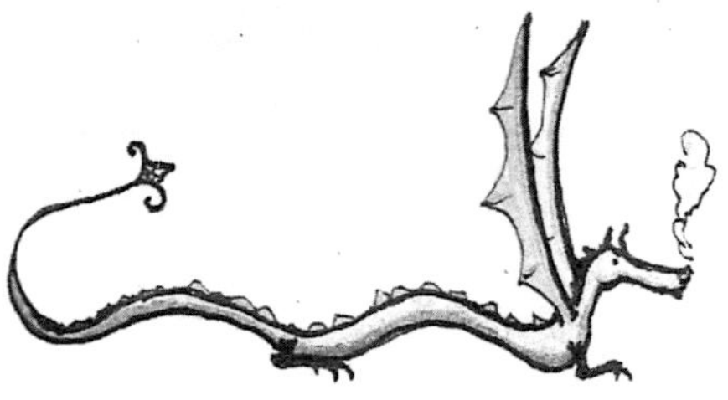

From the look of the recipes in this section, it seems that First Breakfast was a savory affair, meant to kickstart one's day.

Oatcakes

Makes ~a dozen small biscuits   Prep: 5 minutes   Cooking: 30 minutes

This recipe produces crispy little biscuits that are quite plain, but oddly enticing. Ideal for a little savory snack with some cheese or pickle.

Ingredients:

- 1/2 cup all-purpose flour
- 1 cup small flat oats
- 1 tsp baking powder
- pinch of salt
- 3 Tbs. butter, melted
- 2 Tbs. lard, or bacon drippings
- hot water to mix

Combine all the dry ingredients in a bowl, and make a small well in the middle. Pour in the butter and lard, and mix until you have a crumbly texture. Gradually add in hot water, just a little at a time, until the dough becomes a workable consistency.

Roll out the dough to 1/8" thick on a lightly floured surface. You can either cut the oatcakes into triangles or into other shapes with a glass or with cookie cutters. Shift the oatcakes to a baking sheet and bake for 30 minutes at 300°F. Enjoy warm or store in airtight container.

Gravy-poached Eggs

Makes 4-6 servings **Prep: 10 minutes** **Cooking: 30 minutes total**

What could be better than sausage gravy in the morning? What about eggs poached in that same gravy? These poached eggs sit atop a hearty serving of gravy and toast, providing an excellent start to one's day.

Ingredients:

- 4-6 slices of bread
- 1 Tbs. butter
- 1/2 lb. sausages, casings removed, or shredded leftover chicken
- 1/4 cup flour
- 1/2 cup milk
- 2 cups broth
- 4-6 eggs
- salt and pepper

Toast slices of bread, and arrange each on serving plates. Melt butter in a deep frying pan, then cook the sausage in it over medium heat until brown and crumbly. Toss in the flour and combine by stirring for another minute.

Pour in the milk and half the broth, and and continue to stir over medium-low heat as the mixture thickens. After a few minutes, when the mixture has thickened slightly, gently crack an egg into the middle of the pan. Without stirring, let the egg begin to cook, until the bottom of the white is opaque, and beginning to set, which should take a minute or so. Then carefully ladle gravy broth over the top of the egg for about a minute more.

Using a large spoon, carefully scoop up the cooked egg and lay it on the slice of toast. Add a little more gravy around the edges, season to taste, and serve! As you scoop out gravy with each egg, you may need to pour in more of the reserved broth to top off the gravy level. Stir to incorporate each new addition of broth.

Rustic Sausages

Serves: 4 Prep: 10 minutes Cooking: 30 minutes

Shaped by hand, and without casing, these sausages are an easy accompaniment to a savory breakfast. They are richly flavored and just slightly crispy on the outside after frying.

Ingredients:

- 1 lb. of pork
- 1 lb. of lean veal
- 1/2 lb. of beef suet
- 1 cup bread crumbs
- 1/2 tsp. each nutmeg, mace
- 6 sage-leaves, minced
- 1 teaspoonful of pepper
- 2 teaspoonfuls of salt
- 1/2 tsp. each savory or thyme, marjoram
- 1 cup flour
- 1/2 cup oil

Mince the pork and veal, and combine them with the suet, breadcrumbs, spices, and herbs. Mix thoroughly by hand until it is evenly blended. Taking a small handful at a time, form the sausage into slightly flattened oblong shapes. Dip in the flour, and fry in oil over medium heat until the cakes are a nice golden brown, flipping halfway through cooking. Remove to a plate lined with paper towels to drain, then serve warm.

Second Breakfast

Second Breakfast seems to be a sort of dessert to the previous meal, consisting of sweeter dishes and sides of fresh fruits. As if the previous meal weren't enough to successfully start one's day well!

Overnight Porridge

Serves 2-4 **Prep: 5 minutes** **Soaking: ~8 hours** **Cooking: 5 minutes**

This time-saving method of making oatmeal produces a creamy and heartening breakfast dish. Perfect for last-minuted guests, bustling families, or just when you know you'll be in a hurry come morning.

Ingredients:

- 4 cups water
- 1 cup steel cut oats
- 1/2 cup milk
- butter, jam, or other toppings

Bring the water to a boil in a saucepan, then add the oats. Stir gently for a minute, then remove from heat. Cover, and let sit overnight. In the morning, strain out any remaining water, and pour in the milk. Return to heat until warmed through and soft in texture. Serve with butter, jam, fruit, nuts, or your choice of other toppings.

Currant Scones

Makes about 10 scones   Prep: 15 minutes   Cooking: 10 minutes

Soft, flaky, and studded with sweet currants- who could ask for something better for breakfast? These round gems are delicious with a little jam, and even better with a dollop of clotted cream.

Ingredients:

- 1/4 cup dried currants
- 2 cups flour
- 1/4 cup sugar
- 1 Tbs. baking powder
- 1/2 tsp. salt
- 3/4-1 cup cream or milk

Soak the currants in warm water for about 10 minutes, then drain. Combine the currants with the dry ingredients in a bowl, then add the cream a little bit at a time, mixing until you have a soft and workable dough. Press out the dough on a lightly floured surface, folding several times to give the scones layers, then pat out to about 1/2" thick. Cut into rounds using a biscuit cutter or a glass. Place the scones on a baking sheet and bake at 350°F for around 10-15 minutes, or until the tops are just lightly golden.

Custard Sauce

Makes about 1 pint **Prep: 10-15 minutes** **Chilling: at least 6 hours**

Creamy, rich, and decadent, this sauce was made to be savored. Try it with fresh, chilled fruit, or alongside some cake. Dip cookies in it, or eat it with a spoon- it's that good.

Ingredients:

- 2 cups milk or cream
- 2 eggs
- 1/2 cup sugar
- 1 Tbs. brandy
- pinch of nutmeg

Create a double-boiler by setting a medium bowl on top of a small saucepan with about an inch of water at the bottom. The bottom of the bowl should not touch the water. Set on the stove over medium-low heat. Combine the milk, eggs, and sugar in the bowl of the double boiler, and whisk vigorously for several minutes. Continue to whisk gently until the mixture thickens noticeably, around 15 minutes. Remove from heat and stir in the brandy and nutmeg.

Transfer to a clean container, and either serve warm over a hot dessert, or chill until cooled. Consider serving over a variety of fresh fruit, such as berries, apples, grapes, etc.

Custard Sauce

Both the custard and the clotted cream, while delicious, need to be started a day ahead of time, so plan accordingly.

Clotted Cream

Makes about 1 pint | Slow cooking: ~10 hours | Refrigeration: ~8 hours

This recipe produces a smooth and decadent spread that elevates every sort of breakfast baked good. Although it is easy to make, the recipe takes about a full day to prepare, so it's best to start it in the morning, then let it chill overnight.

Ingredients:

- 2 pints heavy cream

Set the oven to the lowest possible setting, usually between 175° and 200°F. Pour the cream into a casserole or other oven-safe dish. Bake for 8-12 hours, then refrigerate for another 8 hours.

Skim the thick cream off the top of the casserole dish and transfer to a clean jar. Reserve the runny cream and use to make scones, or use in baking any other way you normally would use cream or milk.

Serve the set cream with baked goods, fresh fruit, etc. Store in the fridge for up to a week, if there's any left!

view from the top
of the hill

elevensies

In the late morning, one's energy might begin to wane. Thankfully, "Elevensies" was a combination of sweet and savory, and the recipes in this section are lighter, and likely meant for snacking.

Mushrooms on Toast

Serves 4 Prep: 5 minutes Cooking: 10 minutes

This is a fantastic addition to a luncheon spread. The number of recipes and drawings from the collection that involve mushrooms indicates that they were important to this family, and no wonder. That crunch of toast, the soft sweetness of caramelized shallots, rich earthiness of mushrooms and herbs? Delicious.

Ingredients:

- 4 slices of toasted, rustic bread
- 3 Tbs. butter
- 1 large shallot, sliced thin
- 4 oz. mixed mushrooms, (try including shiitake, reishi, or maitake) wiped clean
- 1 clove garlic, minced
- ¼ cup chopped pecans or walnuts
- a few sprigs of fresh thyme, leaves picked
- sea salt
- freshly ground black pepper
- 4 slices of toasted whole-grain sourdough bread
- balsamic vinegar (optional)
- sharp cheese

Melt the butter in a large frying pan over medium heat. Add the garlic and shallots and gently stir until they grow soft. Add the mushrooms, stirring to spread them out. Allow this to cook for a few minutes, until the mushrooms start to soften. Add the walnuts, thyme, salt, and pepper, and continue to cook for about three minutes more.

While the mushroom mixture finishes cooking, arrange your toast slices on serving dishes. When the mushrooms are done, remove the pan from heat, and divide the topping equally between the slices of toast. If you like, drizzle with a little balsamic glaze, then top with cheese while still hot. Serve warm.

Seedcake

Makes 8 servings **Prep: 5 minutes** **Baking: 1 hour**

The brandy and spices are there, but not in a boozy, overwhelming way. In fact, I'd say it has only the good taste of brandy, without the kick. The cake itself is soft and dense, with only the slightest hint of crunch on the outside crust, and imparted by the seeds. Although it would be good with honey or jam, I found that the seedcake itself was good enough to enjoy plain, or with a smidge of butter alongside some afternoon tea.

Ingredients:

- 2 sticks butter (1/2 lb.)
- 3/4 cup sugar
- 1/2 tsp ground nutmeg
- 1/4 tsp ground mace
- 1 Tbs seeds, such as caraway or poppy
- 3 eggs
- 1/4 cup brandy
- 2 cups flour
- 1/2 cup confectioners' sugar
- milk

Cream together the butter and sugar. Add the spices and seeds, followed by the eggs and brandy, beating to combine. Gradually add the flour, stirring until everything is mixed together completely. Pour this thick batter into a tin lined with buttered paper, and bake it at 350°F for 1 hour.

Serve the cake plain, or drizzle with icing: mix just enough milk with the confectioners' sugar to make a pourable consistency. Pour over the cake in a decorative pattern.

Watercress Soup

Serves 4   Prep: 5 minutes   Cooking: 35 minutes

Watercress has a tangy, almost peppery flavor which adds a surprisingly refreshing flavor to soup. It can often be foraged, but is also easy to grow in wet areas, such as ponds and slow flowing streams. This soup is great with a little crusty bread and sharp cheese to accompany it.

Watercress Soup, continued

Ingredients:

- 2 Tbs. butter
- around 4 oz. watercress, washed, coarse stalks removed, chopped
- 1 medium onion, chopped fine
- 2 Tbs. flour
- 1 cup milk
- 2 cups chicken or vegetable stock
- 6 Tbs. heavy cream

Melt the butter in a large pan, then gently fry the onion for a few minuets until softened. Add the watercress and stir for a minute more or so, until wilted. Stir in the flour and cook for another minute. Add in the milk slowly, followed by the stock. Bring to the boil, and stir until thickened. Cover and simmer for 30 minutes. Liquidize, then add the cream and reheat gently without boiling. Serve straightaway.

Westfarthing Rabbit

Makes 2 servings, 4 slices **Cooking: 15 minutes**

Similar to an open-faced grilled cheese, this dish combines cheddar, beer, and mustard, fluffs it up with some egg, then broils the whole thing on slices of toast. The resulting snack provides a wonderful array of textures, from the crunch of the toast to the rich, fluffy give of the topping. The taste is reminiscent of beer mustard on a pretzel, and the choice of a darker rye bread gives the whole dish a wonderfully rich earthiness.

Ingredients:

- 2 Tbs. butter
- 1 shallot, sliced thin
- 1 cup grated cheddar
- 1/3 cup ale or lager
- 1 tsp. mustard
- pinch of salt
- 2 eggs, lightly beaten
- 4 slices of bread, your choice
- black pepper

Melt the butter in a saucepan over medium heat, then add the shallot and cook until it has softened. Add the cheddar, ale, mustard, and salt. Stir over low heat until the cheese has just melted. Add the eggs and stir until the mixture has slightly thickened, around 2 minutes. Be sure to not overcook, or you'll end up with scrambled eggs!

Toast the bread, then spoon the cheesy mixture over the top of the toast. Cook briefly under a hot broiler until the top is puffy and golden. Sprinkle generously with black pepper, and serve.

Apple Tart

Makes 4 medium tarts Prep: 20 minutes Cooking: 20 minutes

Soft pale colors hint at the warmth of this fruity, wondrous dessert. The flavorful sauce pairs beautifully with the tart goat cheese and subtle herbs. It soaks into each colorful curve of baked apple peel, which lie in visual contrast to the straight golden lines of light pastry. It's a delightfully easy recipe to make, which makes it ideal for unexpected houseguests.

Ingredients:

- 1 box frozen puff pastry, thawed
- 1/2 cup dry sherry
- 1/2 cup apple cider or juice
- 1/4 cup honey
- 1 whole sprig rosemary
- 4 large tart apples, cored and sliced thin
- 4 oz. crumbled goat cheese

Combine the sherry, apple cider, honey, and rosemary in a medium saucepan. Add the apples and cook over medium heat until the apples have softened slightly but not lost their shape, about 5-10 minutes, depending on the thickness of the slices. Remove from heat, and strain the apples out, reserving the liquid. Return the liquid to the stove, reduce heat to medium-low. Remove the rosemary and continue to cook until it has thickened slightly, about 15 minutes more.

Slice each sheet of puff pastry into halves, and place on a baking sheet lined with parchment paper. Using a fork, prick the surface of the pastry, leaving a border of 1/2" around the outside edge; this will allow only the outsides to puff up. Sprinkle the goat cheese evenly between the four tarts, then lay the apple slices in a decorative pattern.

Place in the oven and bake for about for 20 minutes at 400°F, or until the outer crust has turned a golden brown. Allow to cool slightly, and drizzle with reserved juice. If you like, garnish with extra rosemary and edible flowers.

Luncheon

And then we come to a midday meal, just in case the first three meals of the day somehow left you wanting. This is a meal that seems well suited to being transported to a picnic, or out to those working in the fields.

Farmer's Cheese

Makes 1 small log Prep: 20 minutes Draining: 8 hours, or overnight

Soft, flavorful, and easy to make, this creamy cheese is wonderful with crisp crackers or slices of fresh apple.

Ingredients:

- 1 quart goat's milk (pasteurized is fine)
- 1/3 cup fresh lemon juice
- salt to taste

You'll also need:

- a sauce pot, preferably stainless steel
- Thermometer
- Cheesecloth
- Strainer or colander
- string or rubberband

Pour the goats milk into the sauce pot. Turn on the heat, and put the thermometer into the milk. When it's reached about 180°F, turn off the heat, and pour in the lemon juice/vinegar and salt. Stir gently to combine, then let sit and cool for around 15 minutes. While the milk is sitting, stretch the cheesecloth over the strainer, and set over another deep bowl or pot. When it's ready, pour the milk mixture into the prepared cheesecloth, letting the liquid drain into the container below. Gather the ends of the cheesecloth together, and secure with string. Hang this bundled cheese over a bowl for at least 2 hours or overnight, until all the liquid has drained out.

At this point, your cheese is done, so work in salt to taste, and form it into a ball or log. Store refrigerated for up to 1 week.

Ploughman's Platter

Serves as many as you like **Prep: minimal**

Imagine spending the morning plowing a field with a sturdy pair of ponies, the satisfaction of creating furrows that will bring forth the bounty of the land. Then imagine the satisfaction of tucking into an emminently satisfying picnic. The real beauty of this meal is that it can be built exactly to your liking.

Suggested Ingredients:

- hearty bread
- cheese, sharp or soft
- apples, grapes, or other fruit
- lettuce or other greens
- pickles
- mustard, chutney, or jam
- boiled eggs
- cured sausage, sliced ham, cold cuts
- carrots, radish, celery
- ale, gingerbeer, etc.

Field Pastries

Makes 8 pastries   Prep: 45 minutes   Baking: 30 minutes

I was baffled by this recipe until I understood the basic concept: a sort of pastry with both savory and sweet fillings, that serves as a meal and dessert in one. Fortunately, there were small sketches of the process in the margins of the original document, from which I was able to work.

Ingredients for:

Dough

- 4 cups flour
- 1 stick butter
- 1 egg yolk divided
- pinch of salt
- 1 ½ cups cold water

Savory Filling

- 3 strips of bacon
- 1 lb. stew beef, cut into bite-sized pieces
- 3 Tbs. flour
- pinch salt & pepper

Sweet Filling

- 2 Tbs. butter
- 2 apples, peeled, cored and diced
- 1/2 cup golden raisins
- 2 Tbs. honey
- splash brandy

Make the dough by rubbing the butter into the dry ingredients. Add the egg yolk, then just enough water to bring it all together. Wrap and chill.

Begin by making the savory filling: fry the bacon in a large pan until crispy. Remove to paper towels to dry. Toss the stew beef with flour, and add to the hot bacon grease. Season with salt and pepper, then cook until all the meat is evenly browned, 5-10 minutes. Crumble the cooled bacon and add back into the beef. Set aside to cool.

Make the sweet filling: Melt the butter in a pan, then add the other ingredients. Cook for around 10-15 minutes, or until the apples are soft. Set aside to cool.

Roll out the chilled dough to around 1/8" thickness. Cut out squares of dough that are roughly 8"x8", reserving the scraps of dough for decorations and to reroll. Gently gather the dough into a raised line about 2/3 of the way across the dough, and pinch it together to hold; This will be the dividing line between your sweet and savory fillings. Spoon ½ cup of the savory mixture onto the larger of the sections of dough, piling it up so it fills roughly ½ of the compartment. Do the same with ¼ cup of the sweet filling on the other side. Carefully fold the top of the dough over the fillings. Wet the edges of the dough with water, then fold the bottom of the dough up over the top, and the sides in, pressing to seal.

To decorate: cut thin strips of dough into pieces roughly 5" long. Pinch the ends of three of these strips together, then braid. Wet the braid with water, then carefully lift a pasty onto it, lining the braid up with the dividing line between the two fillings. Cut out other decorations with small cookie cutters, and attach to the pasties with water. Brush each finished pasty with egg white mixed with a little milk. Bake at 400°F for 30 minutes, or until the tops of the pasties are nice and golden.

Other suggested variations: Duck & Cherry, Pork & Pear, Beef & Plum, Lamb & Berries, Turkey & Cranberry, Chicken & Peach

Pork Pies

Makes one 9" pie, or several smaller pies

Prep: 30 minutes   Cooking: 45 minutes - 1 hour

This pie is at once both hearty and elegant. The salty richness of the pork and cheddar is balanced by the delicate sweetness of the sherry and apples. The leeks provide a delicious understated foundation for the herbs, and the whole combination is held together by a nice flaky crust.

Ingredients for Dough:

- 3 cups flour
- 1 tsp. salt
- 6 Tbs. butter or lard
- 1 cup cold milk

Ingredients for Filling:

- 6 strips of bacon
- 2 leeks
- 2 parsnips, peeled and diced
- 1-2 sprigs each of fresh rosemary and sage (about 1 heaping tsp.)
- 1 cup medium dry sherry
- 1 lb. cubed pork
- 1/2 lb. pork belly, diced
- 1 tsp. salt
- 1/2 cup grated cheddar cheese

Combine the flour and salt. Rub or cut in the butter until the whole mixture has the consistency of fine breadcrumbs. Gradually mix in just enough milk to bring everything together into a nice workable dough. Divide into two sections, one slightly larger than the other. Roll the larger piece out on a lightly floured surface to just about 1/8" thickness. Drape this over a pie pan, and repeat the process with the other section of dough to make the top crust, and set it aside.

Begin by cooking the bacon over medium heat in a large skillet, until the pieces are crispy. Remove the bacon to drain on a plate lined with paper towel. Pour off all but 3 Tbs. of the bacon fat into a separate container. Reduce the heat to medium low, and add the leeks, cooking until they are soft. Add the parsnips and herbs, and stir to coat, cooking for another minute or two. Pour in the sherry, taking care as it can sizzle when it hits the bacon fat. Continue to cook until the parsnips have begun to soften, about 10-15 minutes, then remove from heat and allow to cool completely.

In a separate bowl, mix together the pork and pork belly. Put this mix into a food processor and pulse until the consistency becomes evenly chopped. Mix the bacon back in, as well as the cooled vegetable mixture. Pack this into the prepared pie shell. Drape the top crust over the filled pie, cutting off the excess dough. Fold the edges over and crimp shut.

Bake at 375°F for 45 minutes to an hour, or until the top crust has turned golden and the pork is no longer pink.

If you like, you can also make smaller pies, using a large muffin tin. Follow the same directions as above, and bake for 45 minutes.

Sausage Eggs

Makes: 8 eggs Prep: 15 minutes Cooking: ~30 minutes

Hard-boiled eggs, wrapped in sausage, then fried? Yes please! These hefty treats are protein powerhouses, and their relative portability makes them ideal candidates for inclusion in a picnic basket. Each bite of the crisp savory coating and tender egg will surely satisfy any trekking appetite.

Ingredients:

- 8 medium eggs, hard boiled
- Plain flour, mixed with a pinch each of salt and pepper
- 1 pound sausage meat
- 1 egg, beaten with a dash of water
- Breadcrumbs
- fat or oil, for frying

Peel the eggs and dust with flour mixture. Coat each with sausage meat, keeping it in a good eggy shape. The egg is slippery, so start with a large, flat disc of sausage, then work the edges around to meet one another until the whole egg is covered. Roll the sausaged eggs in flour, then brush with beaten egg, coat with breadcrumbs, and fry in deep fat for about 7 minutes. Place on a plate with paper towels to allow to drain, and allow to cool. Pack into a picnic or serve as part of a cold buffet.

Tea

Some days, a spot of afternoon tea is just the little boost that one needs. In addition to its namesake, this meal is made up of smaller fingerfoods and sweets.

Proper Tea

The making of tea is not so complicated a matter as some might suspect. So long as you have boiling water and enough of the pleasing leaf, then the tea will almost always be good.

To be sure that the tea is extra hot, warm the teapot with boiling water by filling and allowing to sit for several minutes. Then add one spoonful of tea leaves for each person, plus one for the pot, then pour the boiling water over top.

Milk is optional but encouraged for all black teas, but should never be added to herbal or green teas. Sugar or honey may be added to taste, but too much can obscure the flavor of the tea.

Black teas, such as Ceylon, Darjeeling, Assam, and tea blends such as Earl Grey and English Breakfast are all lovely and flavorful options. Looseleaf tea is often superior to our "modern" teabags, which have small bits of leaf to make the water darken quickly, rather than larger leaves for excellent flavor. Herbal tisanes, while not proper tea, can also be quite enjoyable, especially in the evening.

Summer Cake with Strawberries

Serves 12 Prep: 10 minutes Baking: 25-30 minutes

This recipe produces a simple cake that is both light and satisfying, with layers of whipped cream and fresh berries between a fluffy spiced cake. Perfect for warm weather days, it's also an excellent use for strawberries that have gone a bit soft.

Ingredients:

- 2 sticks butter
- 1 cup sugar
- 4 eggs, beaten
- 1/2 tsp. vanilla
- 2 Tbs. milk
- 2 cups flour
- 1 tsp. salt
- 2 Tbs. baking powder
- 1/2 tsp. ground nutmeg
- 1 pint heavy cream
- 8 oz. strawberries, stemmed and sliced
- powdered sugar, to decorate
- extra strawberries, for garnish

Preheat the oven to 375°F. Butter the bottom and sides of two 8" round cake pans.

Cream the butter and sugar together in a large bowl. Add the eggs, vanilla, and milk, mixing until completely combined. In a separate bowl, combine the flour, salt, baking powder, and nutmeg. Gradually fold the dry ingredients into the wet mixture, and tweak the amount of ingredients; you should have a soft, drop-able consistency. Divide the batter evenly between the two tins and bake for 25-30 minutes, until they are golden and somewhat firm to the touch. Gently take the cakes out of the pans, and allow to completely cool on a rack. Once cool, slice each cake into two equal halves, making four total layers.

In a medium bowl, whip the heavy cream until it forms soft peaks. When the cakes are quite cool, begin assembling the cake by sandwiching the layers together using the whipped cream, interspersed with the sliced strawberries. When all the layers are stacked, dust a little powdered sugar on top, and garnish with a few extra strawberries. Because the cake is so tall, best to air on the side of thin slices.

Tea Sandwiches

Makes 16 finger sandwiches **Time: 15 minutes**

Although many varieties exist, my personal favorite small sandwich for teatime is that of cheese and cucumber. What a satisfying cripsness to each bite, with the sharp creaminess of cheese and butter in contrast!

Ingredients:

- 8 slices soft white bread
- 1 English cucumber, sliced very thin
- 4-6 oz. cheddar, thinly sliced
- 4 Tbs. salted butter, softened

Lay out the eight slices of bread. Spread them evenly with the butter, then set four slices aside. Arrange the cucumber slices on top, overlapping where necessary. Place a layer of cheese on top of this, followed by the remaining bread. Press gently downward on each sandwich to help it hold together. With a large and sharp knife, carefully chop off the crusts from the bread. Make two diagonal cuts across the square bread, corner to corner, to create four small sandwich wedges. Set these on a serving plate and repeat with the rest of the sandwiches.

Other delicious varieties: ham, brie, and mustard on toasted bread; pate, capers, and mustard on white; turkey, cheddar, apple, and butter on wheat; roast beef, watercress, with horseradish on rye; smoked trout, cucumber, and butter on pumpernickel; egg salad and parsley on white; lemoncurd and fresh berries on white

Sweet Biscuits

Makes about 20 small biscuits   Prep: 10 minutes Baking: 15 minutes total

These biscuits are ideal for afternoon tea, or to have on hand in case of unexpected company. They are simple, with slight hint of spice and the occasional burst of extra sweetness from the dried fruit, and a bit of crunch from the sugar dusted on top.

Ingredients:

- 1 stick butter, room temperature
- 1/2 cup sugar
- 1 egg, separated
- 1 1/2 cups flour
- 1/2 tsp. ground pie spice
- 1/3 cup dried currants
- 1/4 cup candied peel
- 2 Tbs. brandy or milk
- extra sugar, for sprinkling

Pre-heat oven to 400°F and line a baking sheet with parchment paper. Cream the butter and sugar together until pale and fluffy, then beat in the egg yolk. Sift in the flour and spices and mix well. Add the fruit and peel and enough brandy or milk to make a fairly soft dough. Knead lightly on a lightly floured surface and roll out until about 1/4 inch thick, prick the tops with a fork and cut into 4" rounds or other desired shapes. Place on prepared baking sheets, bake for 10 minutes. Remove from the oven, brush with the lightly beaten egg white, sprinkle with sugar and return to the oven to bake for about 5 minutes longer, until the tops are golden brown. Transfer to wire racks to cool. Store in an airtight container.

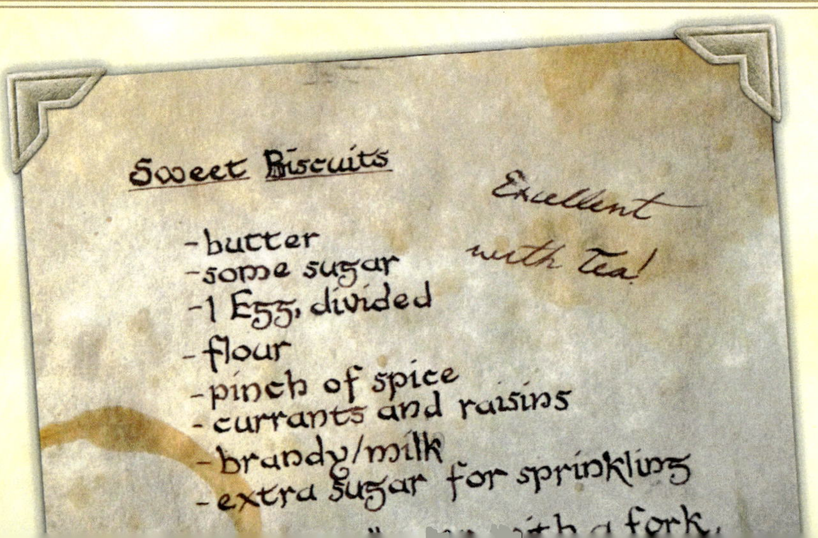

Chamomile Tea

Makes 1-2 mugs of tea   Steeping: 2 minutes

This herbal tea comforts the spirit as much as it relaxes the body. The combination of flowers and fruit, along with a dash of honey, invokes the feeling of sunny summer afternoons.

Ingredients:

- ~2 cups boiling water
- 1 heaping Tbs. dried chamomile
- pinch of lavender
- slice of apple
- honey, to taste

Combine chamomile, lavender, and apple in a tea strainer. Pour boiling water over, steep for around two minutes, then sweeten to taste with honey.

Wildflower honey is great, but heavier honey, as from buckwheat, adds character
ONE MATHOM
Simbelmynë

Dinner

Dinner appears to be an evening equivalent of First Breakfast- it is made of mostly simple, hearty fare appropriate for every-day eating.

Country Loaf

Serves 4 Prep: 10 minutes Rising: 1 1/2 hours Baking: 30 minutes

This recipe makes such a light and fluffy bread that it's difficult to stop eating it, especially when still warm from the oven. The interesting shape might be an elegant solution to baking in narrow ovens- go vertical!

Ingredients:

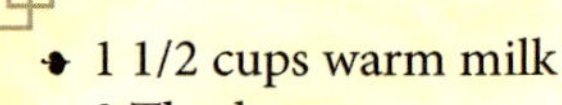

- 1 1/2 cups warm milk
- 2 Tbs. honey
- 2 tsp dried yeast
- 3 cups white flour
- 2 Tbs. butter, melted
- 1 tsp. salt
- beaten egg to glaze

In a medium sized bowl, combine the warm milk, honey, and the yeast, and allow to sit for about 5 minutes, until frothy. Add the salt, followed by half the flour, and the butter. Gradually add the remaining flour until the dough comes together and pulls away from the side of the bowl. Tip the dough out onto a lightly floured surface, and knead for a few minutes, until it bounces back when poked. Place in a greased bowl and cover with a tea towel. Allow to rise for about an hour, or until doubled in size. Punch the dough back down.

Preheat the oven to 425°F. Take about 1/3 of the dough and form into a round, pulling the sides down around the bottom until you're left with a nice smooth shape. Do the same with the remaining dough and place it on a lightly greased baking sheet. Place the smaller round on top of the larger one. With the lightly floured or oiled handle of a wooden spoon, poke a hole down the center of the two stacked rounds- this will help keep them together. Cover and allow to rise for another 30 minutes, then brush with the beaten egg. Bake for 30 minutes. Allow to rest for 10 minutes to cool before cutting into.

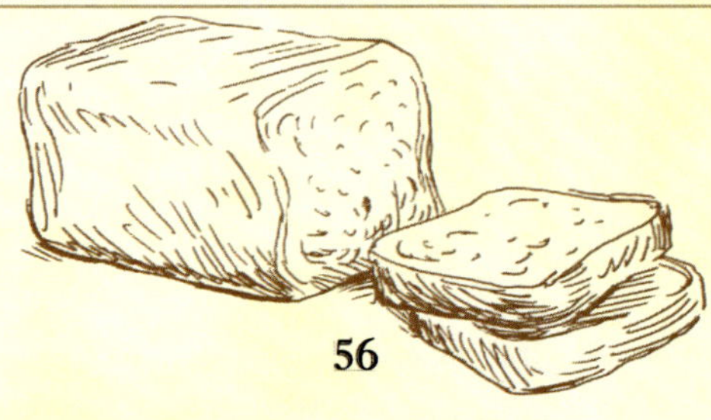

Mushroom Soup

Makes 4 servings Prep: 10 minutes Cooking: 45 minutes

Incredibly rich and creamy, a little of this soup goes a long way. The beef broth and smoked salt bring out the earthiness of the mushrooms, while the cheese and cream add to the wonderful texture. Consider serving with some crusty white bread to soak up every bit of soup from the bowl.

Ingredients:

- 2 Tbs. butter
- 1 large onion, diced
- 1-2 cloves garlic, minced
- 4 oz. shitake mushrooms, roughly chopped
- 10 oz cremini mushrooms, roughly chopped
- 2 cups beef broth
- 1 tsp. smoked salt
- 1 cup cream
- 1 Tbs. sherry
- 1/3 cup finely shredded sharp cheddar, plus more for garnish

Melt the butter in a saucepan, add the onion and garlic, then cook until they are softened but not yet brown. Add the chopped mushrooms and stir to coat them with butter. Cover with broth and cream, add the salt, and bring to just under a simmer for 30 minutes.

Using a slotted spoon, scoop out 1/2 cup of the cooked mushrooms and onions, and set aside as a garnish. Puree the rest of the soup using either a submersible blender or an upright blender. When the texture is smooth and creamy, add the sherry and the grated cheese, then stir to combine.

Scoop into bowls, garnish with the reserved mushrooms if desired, and shred a little extra cheese over the top.

Roast Chicken

Serves 4 Prep: 10 minutes Cooking: 1 ½ hours

This chicken is a filling dish that's simple to make, yet savory and satisfying. The skin crisps in the oven to a beautiful golden brown. I serve this with a selection of root vegetables, such as potatoes and carrots. If scattered around the bird, and occasionally tossed with the fat, they cook along with the chicken. The stuffing is satisfying, salty from the bacon, flavored with the juice from the poultry.

Ingredients:

- 1 chicken, about 5 lb.
- 2 Tbs. butter, divided
- 2-3 shallots, diced
- 2 cups stale bread, torn small
- 4 strips streaky bacon, 2 chopped & 2 cut in half
- 1 Tbs. fresh parsley, chopped
- 1 egg, beaten
- Salt and black pepper
- 2-4 carrots or parsnips, sliced
- 1 medium potato, cut into chunks

Melt 1 Tbs. butter in a saucepan, and fry the diced shallots over medium height until they are soft, around 2 minutes. Add the cooked shallots and butter to the other stuffing ingredients- bread, chopped bacon, parsley, and egg. Spoon this stuffing into the chicken. Melt the other tablespoon butter and rub it all over the outside of the bird. Sprinkle with salt and pepper, then lay the four short strips of bacon over the breast. Tuck the wings underneath the bird to prevent them from burning. Settle the prepared chicken in a roasting pan, and surround with vegetables. Cook at 400°F for 1 1/2 hours, or until the juices run clear. A little before the end of cooking, remove the strips of bacon to allow the breast to brown.

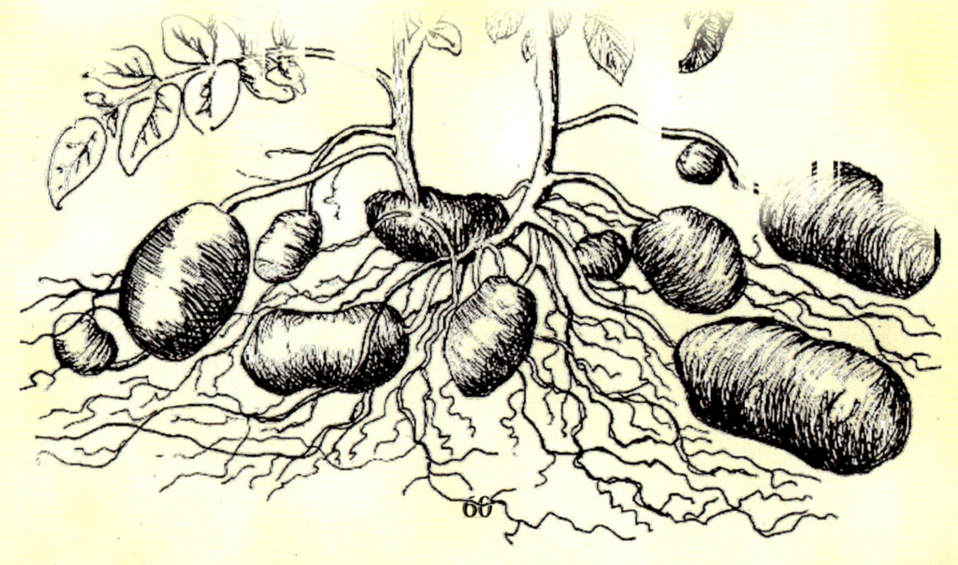

Roast 'Taters

Serves 4-6 Prep: 15 minutes Baking: 45 minutes

Roast 'taters are a terrific accompaniment to any roast meat, providing a starchy counterpart to the rich protein. The original page containing this recipe was spattered and worn, indicating that this was a favorite amongst the collection.

Ingredients:

- 2 lb roasting potatoes, cut into 1 1/2" pieces
- Boiling water
- 1/4 cup vegetable or olive oil
- coarse salt

Preheat the oven to 425°F. Fill a large pot halfway with water, and bring to a boil. Add the potatoes, and simmer for 10 minutes. Drain the water from the pot, pour in the oil, then put the lid back on. Shake the pot a few times to soften the outside of the potatoes, which will make them crispier while cooking.

Transfer the potatoes to a roasting pan, sprinkle with salt, and bake for around 45 minutes, or until they are a pretty golden color and crispy.

Gaffer's Blackberry Tart

Makes 4-6 small tarts   Prep: 1 hour   Baking: 20 minutes

Very simple, yet filling. There are notes on the side of the original document indicating that "Blackberrying" was a much anticipated event of the year. Since the berries themselves are only briefly baked, they hold their shape, making for a beautiful showcake of summer bounty.

Ingredients for Pastry:

- 1 ¼ cups all-purpose flour
- 2 Tbs. sugar
- ¼ tsp. salt
- 1 stick cold unsalted butter
- ¼ cup cold water

Ingredients for Filling:

- 12 oz. blackberries
- 1/2 pint blackberry jam
- 1/2 cup sliced nuts, such as almonds or walnuts

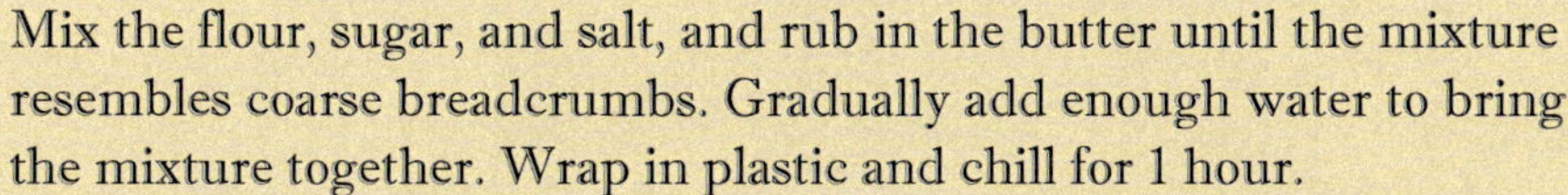

Mix the flour, sugar, and salt, and rub in the butter until the mixture resembles coarse breadcrumbs. Gradually add enough water to bring the mixture together. Wrap in plastic and chill for 1 hour.

Preheat the oven to 375°F. Roll out the chilled dough to around 1/8" thick. Press into tart pans and mold the dough to the sides. Trim the extra and reroll until all the dough is used up. Prick the bottoms of the tart shells all over with a fork, which will keep the dough from bubbling up. Bake for 15 minutes, until the shells are golden brown.

Take the tart shells out of the oven, and immediately spread the jam evenly amongst all the tarts. Place the blackberries in the tarts, sprinkle with almonds, and bake for another 5 minutes. Serve warm or **cold.**

Supper

Here we have a showcase of rich, somewhat decadent dishes that beautifully showcase quality ingredients. These dishes are suitable for special occasions.

Stewed Coney

Serves 4 **Prep: 15 minutes** **Cooking: 1 hour**

This is a wonderful dish with savory autumnal flavors. The cider gives the broth some sweetness, but the apple flavors compliment the rabbit nicely. The salty dumplings are delicious, soaked with broth and scooped up with bits of meat and vegetable.

Ingredients for Stew:

- 4 strips bacon
- 2 rabbits
- 2 leeks
- 2 medium carrots
- 1 large parsnip
- (1/2 lb. small onions)
- 2 cups apple cider
- 3 cups water
- 1 15 oz. can beans, such as butter, broad, fava, etc.
- 1 Tbs. chopped fresh sage
- 1 tsp. fresh thyme
- 2 bay leaves
- generous pinch salt

Ingredients for Dumplings:

- 2 cups flour
- 3 Tbs. baking powder
- 1 tsp. salt
- 1/4 cup butter
- milk, to mix

In a medium saucepan, fry the bacon until it starts to crisp, then remove to cool on a plate, reserving the fat. Brown the rabbit in the bacon grease, then remove to the same plate. Add the garlic and vegetables to the pan, toss to coat in grease, then add a splash of water, cover, and let simmer until soft, about 10-15 minutes. Add this and remaining stew ingredients to a large pot, cover, and simmer for 45 minutes.

Mix all dry ingredients for the dumplings, then gradually add milk until you have a soft, dropable dough. Drop in large dollops on top of the stew, then replace the lid and cook until the dough has risen and is cooked through, about 15 minutes.

Dish with Mushrooms and Bacon

Serves 2 Prep: 5 minutes Cooking: 15 minutes

You can't ask for an simpler or` tastier side dish. Fantastic flavors of savory sage and salty bacon cover the tender mushrooms, blending deliciously with their earthiness.

Ingredients:

- 8 oz. mixed mushrooms
- 2 strips bacon, diced
- 1 heaped Tbs. fresh sage, thinly sliced
- pinch of salt

Combine all ingredients. Bake at 350°F for 15 minutes, stirring occasionally to coat the mushrooms with bacon grease. Serve hot.

Trout with Butter

Serves 2 Prep: 10 minutes Cooking: 10 minutes

This is a recipe that produces a flaky, lightly seasoned fish that is easy to cook and even easier to enjoy. The white wine compliments the fish, especially as the remainder of the bottle can be enjoyed with the meal.

Ingredients:

- 2 trout, about 1/2 lb. each
- pinch of salt
- 1 sprig each fresh thyme and marjoram
- 3 bay leaves
- 2 cups white wine
- water
- lemon (optional)

Place the trout in a large frying pan. Sprinkle them with salt, and add the herbs to the pan. Pour in the white wine, then just enough water to slightly cover the fish.

Bring the liquid to a slow boil over medium high heat, then reduce to a simmer. Allow to cook for about five minutes, then flip both fish. Cook for another three minutes, then remove from heat. Carefully lift each fish out of the pan, allowing it to drip for a few seconds. Garnish with lemon slices, or consider serving with a dollop of the fantastic herbed butter from the back of the book.

Braised Lamb Shanks

Serves 2 Prep: 10 minutes Cooking: 3 hours

This recipe produces a dish that lets the delicious flavors of the lamb shine through. Braised until tender, the meat itself all but falls from the bone, while the savory sauce bursts with extra flavor.

Ingredients:

- 2 Lamb Shanks
- 3 carrots, peeled, rough chopped
- 4 cloves garlic, sliced
- 1 Bay leaf
- 2 tsp. mixed herbs 1 onion, cut into eighths
- 1 cup red wine
- 2 cups beef broth

Heat a medium sized saucepan with tall sides over medium heat. Season lamb shanks and sear each side in the pan. Add the red wine, veggies, and herbs, then pour in the beef broth. Add enough water to just cover the shanks, then cover and allow to simmer for 1 1/2 hours.

Preheat the oven to 350°F. Transfer the shanks, veggies, and juices to an ovenproof dish, cover loosely with foil, and cook for another 1 1/2 hours. When they are done, remove the shanks and veggies and keep them warm. Discard the bay leaves. Pour the juices back into a saucepan, add the butter, and reduce until you have a thickened sauce.

Plate the shanks, and pour the sauce over to serve.

Brandy Snaps

Makes at least two dozen snaps **Prep: 45 minutes**

The brandy snap is a fabulous, simple, yet decadent little dessert. The wafers crunch with a dark sweetness, full with the flavors of warm spices, and filled with the lightest slightly boozy cream.

Ingredients for Wafers:

- 1 stick Butter
- 1/2 cup Molasses
- 1/4 cup Sugar
- 1/4 cup Brown Sugar
- 1 Tablespoon Brandy
- 3/4 cups Flour
- 1/8 teaspoon Salt
- 1/4 teaspoon Ground Ginger

Ingredients for Filling:

- 2 cups Heavy Cream
- 1/3 cup Sugar
- 2 Tablespoons Brandy (more To Taste)

Line two baking sheets with parchment paper or a silicone sheet, and preheat the oven to 350°F. Sift together the flour, salt, and spices, and set aside. Have several wooden-handled spoons handy.

Melt together the butter, molasses, and sugars in a small saucepan over medium heat. Stir gently until the sugar has dissolved, then remove from the heat.

Drop a teaspoon at a time of the batter onto the prepared baking sheets, leaving about 4" of space between each. When the sheet is full, bake for a scant 5 minutes, until each drop has spread out and is bubbly. Remove the tray from the oven. Carefully peel each disc from the sheet and wrap around the handle of one of the spoons to shape into a tube. Slip off the spoon and place onto a cooling rack. If the discs harden before shaping, return to the oven briefly to soften again.

When you are ready to serve, whip the heavy cream with the sugar until it forms peaks. Add the brandy and beat for another minute. Transfer the whipped cream into a piping bag fitted with a decorative tip. Squeeze the whipped cream into each tube and serve immediately.

The shaped and unfilled wafers can be kept in an airtight container for several days.

Mince Pies

Makes about a dozen mini pies **Prep: 20 minutes** **Baking: 20 minutes**

If the wintery holiday season could be put into a single pastry, it would taste an awful lot like these little delicacies. Heavy, spiced, and dense, each bite is full of exciting flavors and textures.

Ingredients for Pastry:

- 2 1/2 cups flour
- 1 stick butter
- pinch salt
- 2 Tbs. sugar, plus more for dusting
- ~1 cup cold milk

Ingredients for Filling:

- 2 cups currants
- 2 cups golden raisins
- 4 Tbs. butter, melted
- 1 cup mixed candied peel
- 1 cup dried currants
- 3 Tbs. brandy
- 1/2 cup brown sugar
- 1/2 tsp. each ginger, cinnamon, nutmeg
- pinch of ground cloves
- 1/2 apple, peeled and diced
- 1 lemon, juiced and zested

Make the dough by combining the dry ingredients in a bowl, then rubbing or cutting in the butter until the mixture resembles dry breadcrumbs. Gradually add in the milk until the dough pulls together. Set aside.

Combine all ingredients for the filling, and let sit in the refrigerator until ready. It can be stored for up to a week.

Preheat oven to 400°F. Roll out dough to 1/8" thick, cut out circles and put in a patty pan, or small/shallow muffing tin. Cut the same number of tops with a decorative shape. Fill with mincemeat, put tops on, crimping edges with a bit of water. Brush milk over each and sprinkle lightly with sugar. Bake for 20 minutes, and remove from tin while still hot, then cool on a wire rack.

a special yuletide treat, these mince pies are a must during the holiday season. combine half pound currants, half pound sultanas, som butter and mixed peel, a few jiggers brandy, some brown sugar, pinch ginger, cinnamon, nutmeg, pinch of ground cloves, a little apple

miscellany

These recipes didn't seem to belong in any of the other categories. Some are simply condiments, or beverages, but others are more eclectic and interesting...

Twice-Baked Honeycakes

Prep: 10 minutes **Baking: 45 minutes** **Caramel: 15 minutes**

Makes about two dozen small honeycakes

Twice-baked for durability, and full of tasty morsels to give you energy, these honeycakes are wonderful traveling companions. They are made with ingredients from the forest and fields, and just bite-sized enough to be a temptation. If you aren't packing these little cakes up to take with you, consider drizzling them with a bit of honey caramel- it adds to their presentation and the flavor can't be beat!

Ingredients for Honeycakes:

- 3 eggs
- 2/3 cup honey
- 1 tsp. dried lavender
- 1 Tbs. dried chopped rosehips
- 2 1/4 cups flour
- 1-1/2 tsp. hartshorn, or baking powder
- 1 tsp. salt
- 1/2 cup dried cherries or berries
- 1/4 cup walnuts, roughly chopped

Heat oven to 350F. In a large bowl, whisk together the honey and eggs until they are a light golden color. Mix in the lavender and rosehips, followed by the flour and the baking powder. When the dough has pulled together, knead in the dried berries and nuts until they are evenly distributed. Divide the dough into three sections, and on a lined baking sheet, form into logs about 3" across and 7" long, patting them down to a height of under 1". Bake logs for 20 minutes, until just slightly golden and somewhat firm to the touch. Remove from oven and allow to cool for 10 minutes. Turn the oven down to 275°F. Cut logs diagonally into 1/2" slices, then lay these back on the baking sheet.

Bake again for 12 minutes, then flip and bake for another 12 minutes. The outsides should be slightly crisp.

Hartshorn was a predecessor to baking powder, and was literally made of ground antlers

Ingredients for Caramel:

- 1 cup Honey
- 3/4 cup Heavy Cream
- 2 Tablespoons Butter

Combine honey and cream in a sauce pan and bring to a boil. Stir occasionally while it cooks. Continue cooking until the mixture reaches soft ball stage, or 240°F; The easiest way to do this is with a candy thermometer. Remove pan from the heat and immediately add the butter, stirring until butter is completely melted and combined. While still warm, drizzle over the baked and cooled honeycakes.

Waybread

Makes ~20 pieces | Prep: 10 minutes | Baking: 20 minutes

This is one of the more curious recipes in the collection. It seems to be intended for travel, so the ingredients are high in protein for maximum nutrients. The flavor is quite unique. Between the elderflower, honey, and fresh thyme, the sweet and savory blend with one another, creating a subtle taste experience. They are filling, yet strangely enticing. I have to think that the "original" of which the recipes speaks, would have been a different dish altogether.

Ingredients:

- 1/2 cup Butter
- 1/2 cup Honey
- 1-2 tsp. minced fresh thyme
- 2 tsp. dried elderflower
- 2 cups All-Purpose Flour
- 1 cup oat flour
- 1/2 cup nut flour, such as chestnut, hazelnut, acorn, or almond
- 1/4 cup hot water
- large fresh leaves, about 20
- grass or twine, for tying

Beat butter and honey in large bowl until mixture is light and fluffy. Add the elderflower and thyme and work into the mix. Gradually add the flours, beating well after each addition. If dough becomes too stiff to stir, knead in remaining flour by hand. Work in the nuts.

Roll out to 1/2" thick on a parchment lined baking sheet. Bake at 300°F for 20 minutes, or until slightly golden. Cut into squares while still warm. Allow to cool, then wrap in leaves of your choice- Sassafras leaves work especially well.

Apple Jelly

Makes roughly 2 pints jelly **Prep: 20 minutes** **Cooking: 45 minutes, or longer**

Here's a jelly that embodies all the goodness of autumnal harvest, and it couldn't be easier to make. The resultant spread is flavorful and sweet.

Ingredients:

- 2 dozen apples, or 6 cups fresh apple juice
- 3 cups honey
- cinnamon or ginger (optional)

Cut apples into quarters, peel, and core. Boil the apples, and spices, if using, until the apples break down. into mush. Strain this to get the juice. Measure out the juice- use 1/2 cup honey for every cup of juice. Boil until it reaches around 220°F, or will gel on a cold plate.

Either can using all the appropriate procedures and precautions, or store in the fridge for up to two weeks.

Raspberry Jam

Makes about 1 1/2 cups jam   Prep: 5 minutes   Cooking: 20 minutes

This simple jam is an ideal addition to scones and clotted cream. The fruit is lightly complimented by the citrusy lemon balm, just sweet enough.

Ingredients:

- 12 oz. raspberries (1 quart)
- 1 cup sugar
- 2 Tbs. lemon balm, cut into thin sliver

Put the raspberries, sugar, and lemonbalm into a small saucepan, and gently warm over medium heat. Mash the berries against the bottom of the pan, and continue to cook for about 15 minutes, until the sugar has completely dissolved. If you would like less seedy a jam, strain out some of the seeds and pour the pulp back into the pan.

Either can using all the appropriate procedures and precautions, or store in the fridge for up to two weeks.

Herbed Butter

Makes 1/2 lb. **Prep: 15 minutes**

Herb-infused butter is a wonderful way to spruce up just about any dish, but it's especially good when you let the butter shine, say on a piece of toast.

Ingredients:

- 2 sticks butter (1/2 lb), softened
- 1/2 cup fresh herbs, whole
- 2 cups boiling water
- dash of salt

Place the herbs in a medium heat-proof bowl, and pour the boiling water over them. This blanching helps lock in that lovely green color. Carefully fish out the herbs with a fork, and pat dry with paper towel.

When they are cool, take the leaves of the herbs off their stems, and slice very thinly. Using a spoon or a flexible knife, gradually work the herbs and salt into the softened butter. When it's all evenly combined, form into a log shape. You can either store in the fridge for immediate use, or wrap in wax paper and slip into a freezer bag for later enjoyment. When you are ready to use, simply slice a bit of butter off the log and allow to come to room temperature.

NOTE: Almost any herb is a delicious addition to butter, but my favorites include thyme, savory, sage, and dill. If you are lucky enough to have access to wild ramps in the spring, they make one of the best compound butters that exists. Ingredients like shallots, capers, and other strong flavors can also be added. Experiment!

Forest Draught

Each recipe makes about 1 cup **Prep: 30 minutes**

The flavor of both draughts is unique, unlike anything I've tasted before. They have hints of familiar flavors, but presented in a wholly new way. Despite being dark tea-based brews, the finished draughts are as clear as a forest stream. The odd recipe notes that while it "cannot promise to make you grow", it approximates the original drink. The small amount of beverage this produces certainly reminds one of cool forests and breezes through the country...

Ingredients for Light Version:

- 6 cups water
- 1/2 cup loose green or white tea leaves
- 1/2 sprig fresh rosemary
- 3 mint leaves
- 2 Tbs. chamomile
- 1 Tbs. dried roses
- lots of ice

Ingredients for Earthy Version:

- 6 cups water
- 4 black tea bags
- 1 sprig thyme
- 1 Tbs. heather tips
- 1 tsp. peat-smoked barley
- lots of ice (at least 6 trays worth...)

Combine all ingredients in a large saucepan with a lid. Warm slightly. Place a heatproof bowl in the center of the pot; make sure it is tall enough to stay above the water level. Turn the lid of the pot upside down and place it on the pot. This will enable the distilled vapors to run down the lid and collect in the bowl. Cover the lid with ice, and bring to a low simmer. Keep on the heat until most of the liquid has evaporated. The first version should be served chilled, the second at room temperature.

Apple Beer

Makes about one gallon **Prep: 1 hour** **Fermenting: 1 month, minimum**

The taste of this is... unusual. The apple elements are there, which makes one expect it to be sweet. But it's a beer, so it's decidedly beery. It pours out very fizzy, but the head doesn't last long. As it sits, a layer of malt sediment settles to the bottom of the glass. It has a sour element and a slightly thick consistency.

Ingredients:

- 1 1 gallon sweet apple cider
- 2.5 lb. light malt mix
- 6 cups boiling water (for sparge)
- .2 oz. hops, at 15 minutes to end of boil
- yeast
- .06 lb. sugar to prime

Heat cider to about 150°F, and add the malt, preferably in a straining bag. Soak the grains at the temperature for 45-60 minutes, then remove, squeezing to extract as much liquid as possible.

Sparge with 6 cups boiling water, and squeeze again to remove liquid. Reserve the spent grains for baking.

Boil the liquid for 30 minutes or so, adding in the hops and the Irish moss near the end. Strain and let cool, then pour into your carboy. When cooled, pitch the yeast and cap with an airlock. Allow to ferment until finished, a month at least, then rack off the lees and into sterilized bottles. Enjoy after another month, and within one year of bottling.

Horselord Mead

Makes just under 1 gallon

Prep: 1 hour Fermenting: 3-4 months Aging: 2 months, minimum

This is a curious brewing recipe. Based on the number of equine-affiliated ingredients, it seems to have been developed by a culture that highly valued their horses. The resulting brew is still semi-sweet, unique and flavorful, with pleasant horsey hints.

Ingredients:

- 3 lb. honey
- 1/2 cup dried lingonberries
- 1 heaping Tbs. horsetail herb
- 1/2 Tbs. elecampane (aka Horse-heal)
- 1 tsp. Ashwaghanda
- 2 Tbs. dried linden leaves
- 1/4 cup dried clover blossoms
- 2 heaped Tbs. meadowsweet
- Nottingham Ale yeast

Place the lingonberries in a separate cloth bag to keep them apart from the herbs, and easier to retrieve later. Combine everything, plus a half gallon of water, in a large pot. Warm over low heat for 15 minutes, until the honey is dissolved. Remove the berries, and strain the liquid into a gallon carboy. When cool, pitch the yeast, add the berries back in, and allow to ferment until finished, around three to four months. Rack as needed. Bottle with all due caution, and age at least 2 months.

White Mead of the Elves

Makes just under 1 gallon

Prep: 1 hour Fermenting: 3-4 months Aging: 1 month, minimum

One of the really unique elements of this brew is that an egg white is boiled into the wort near the beginning of the brewing process, resulting in a very pretty and crystal clear finished mead. The herbal and floral flavors are there, giving it an unexpected complexity.

Ingredients:

- water
- 3.5 lb. honey
- 1 egg white
- 3 Tbs. each lemon balm, hyssop
- 2 Tbs. each clover flowers, linden, dried rosehips, marjoram
- 1 Tbs. thyme, whole hops
- 1 heaping cup dried elderflowers
- 1/2 cup chopped white raisins

Combine the honey and 1 gallon of water. Bring to a boil while stirring to make sure the honey doesn't stick to the bottom and singe. Add the beaten egg white, while whisking. The white should cook, and rise to the top, carrying with it any impurities from the honey. Skim off anything that rises.

Simmer herbs in 2/3 gallon of the sweetened water for 15 minutes, then remove from heat and let sit for another 15. Strain out the herbs, and allow the liquid to cool somewhat. Pour into a carboy, and pitch yeast when it's cool enough. When the mead is done fermenting, bottle with appropriate caution and age at least a month.

For my parents,
who gave me a great love of fantastical realms,
usually let me read by flashlight after bedtime,
and almost always forgive the near disastrous
state of my kitchen...

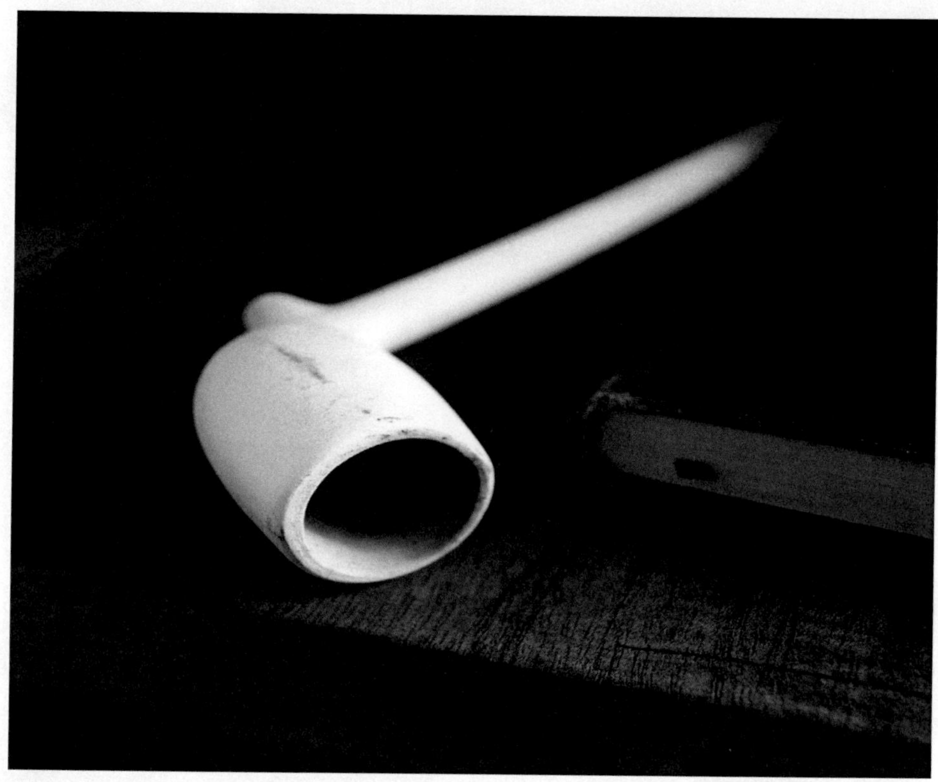

The best books tell stories; like all my favorites, this one is a work of fantasy. The premise: that a box of documents and other tidbits mysteriously made the jump from a fictional world into an attic in our own. Attics are, after all, curious things. That box, with its assortment of odds and ends, eventually passed through the generations to my grandmother, then to me. Herein, you'll find what the finished compilation would look like, bound up like a scrapbook, with several generations of photographs and notes.

It's perfectly fine to simply use this as you would a normal cookbook. But if you are looking for more, it's there, along with a few Shire lessons for living a better life: Cherish your friends. Be generous. Welcome unexpected visitors. Don't be hasty. Plant seeds. Tell stories. Be polite to trees. Hope, always.

I like to imagine that such a fiction is possible, and that those short, happy eaters are still living in a secluded bit of countryside, set apart from the bustle of the modern world.

-Chelsea

17th June, 1932.

My dearest M,

You'll never imagine what I found at the church rummage sale on Monday last.

Underneath a ratty old fur coat, (which old Mrs. Hamm was eyeing, you can be sure), I found a curious wooden box, which must have been very handsome when it was new. Many long years must have passed between now and then though, (don't they for all of us?) I nearly let it pass me by when Liza Hornby demanded half a crown for it, (trying to cheat me as usual,) but she took two shillings in the end.

Upon arriving home, I began to explore my new acquisition. The box appeared to contain only a few knicknacks: a pipe, some musty old tobacco, and a dry inkwell. But the real treasure lay in a hinged compartment behind a pretty little map (labeled "the Shire") engraved on the inside of the lid: a selection of old recipes and several pages of botanical notes, old letters, and other assorted papers. There are some oddities though. The recipes are organized into no fewer than seven different meals: First Breakfast, Second Breakfast, Elevensies, Luncheon, Tea, Dinner, and Supper. I struggle to imagine the constitution of the folk who ate so heartily.

Still, the dishes look tasty, and well worth a bit of experimentation. Knowing your enthusiasm for old recipes, I immediately thought of you, and resolved to send the lot your way.

I cannot help but wonder, however, who were these country-dwellers, with their prodigious appetites? Where is this "Shire" on the map? Perhaps you can puzzle it out.

Do try to come for a visit, when next you are able. It would be so good to see you again, and to finally meet your young Tom.

I remain ever,
your friend,

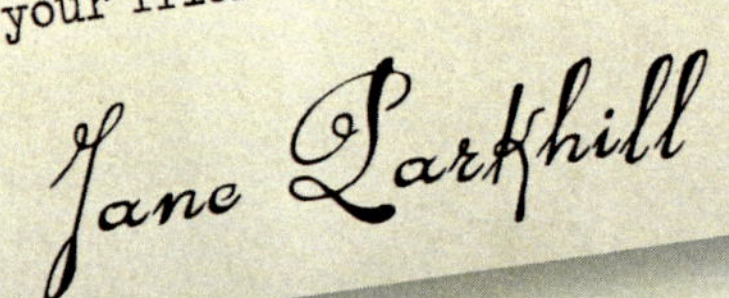

These photographs show some of the original documents as well as the box in which they were discovered.

But all the while, I sit and think of times there were before,

I listen for returning feet and voices at the door.

~J.R.R. Tolkien

Table of Contents

First Breakfast

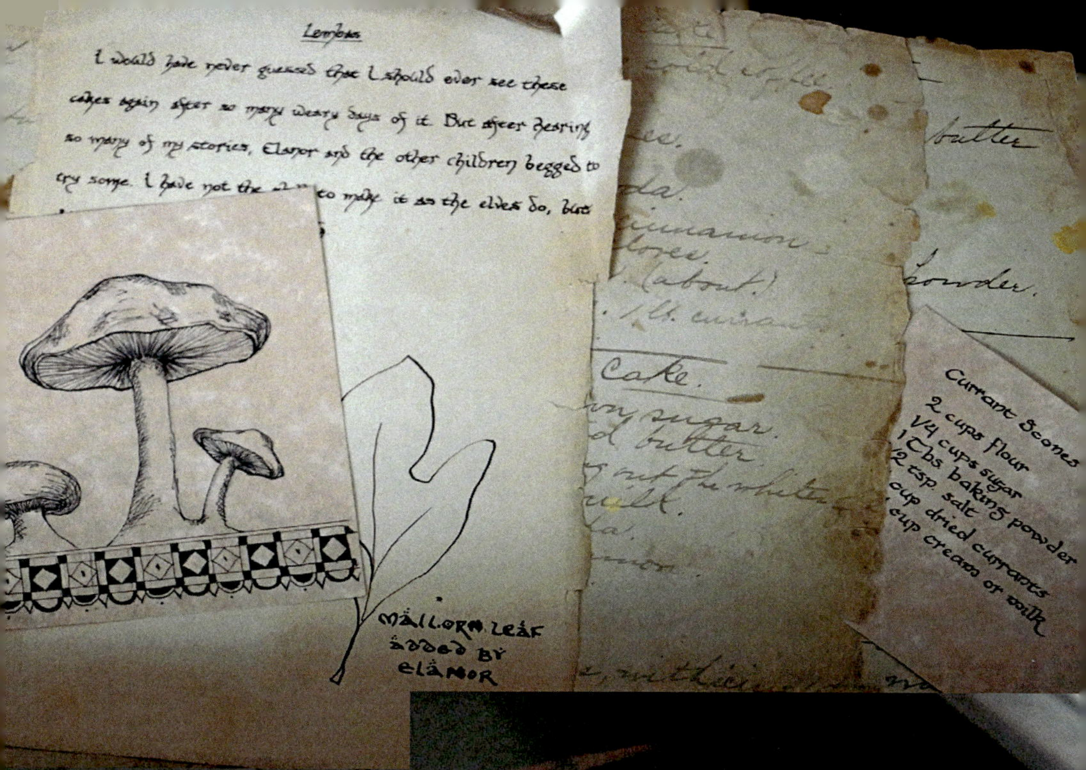

Lembas

I would have never guessed that I should ever see these cakes again after so many weary days of it. But after hearing so many of my stories, Elanor and the other children begged to try some. I have not the ... to make it as the elves do, but

MALLORN LEAF ADDED BY ELANOR

Cake.

Currant Scones
2 cups flour
1/4 cups sugar
1 Tbs baking powder
1/2 tsp salt
cup dried currants
cup cream or milk

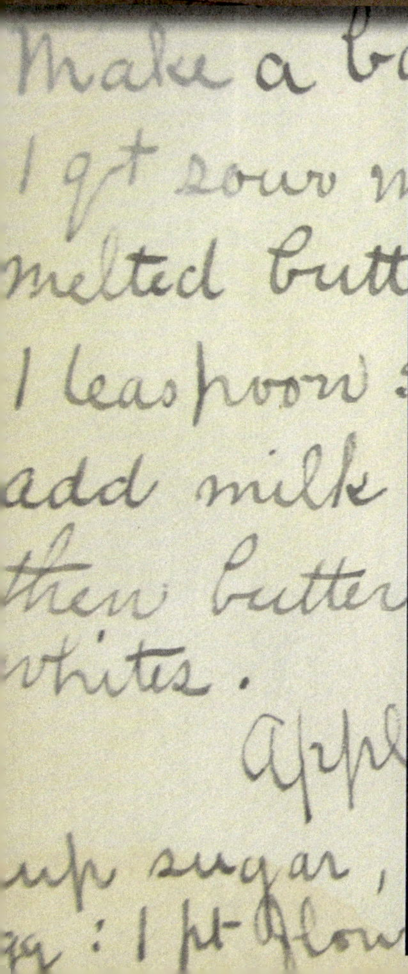

Make a b
1 qt sour m
melted butt
1 teaspoon
add milk
then butter
whites.

Appl
up sugar,
gg : 1 pt flour

Index by Meal

Soups:

Sides, Snacks, & Smaller Dishes:

Mains:

Sweets:

Condiments & Sauces:

Drinks:

A note on Citations

In the process of writing this cookbook, I have made every effort to thoroughly research the recipes. Some come directly from Tolkein's works, others are based on popular recipes from the decades and regions that were the basis for Hobbiton.

Tolkien wrote that

> *"'The Shire' is based on rural England and not any other country in the world… There is no special reference to England in the 'Shire' — except of course that as an Englishman brought up in an 'almost rural' village of Warwickshire on the edge of the prosperous bourgeoisie of Birmingham (about the time of the Diamond Jubilee!) I take my models like anyone else — from such 'life' as I know." (Tolkien's Letters, 250 #190, 235 #181)*

This puts the Shire around the late 1890s in rural England. When possible, I have used historical recipes contemporaneous to that period, predominantly those drawn from Mrs. Beeton's Book of Household Management, originally published in 1861. I have also explored traditional dishes from the areas where Tolkien lived and worked.

Thus, every recipe fits into one of three categories:

Canon - dishes that were specifically mentioned in the books

Inferred - dishes made with listed ingredients, fitting the aesthetic and rough time period

Regional - dishes from places where Tolkien lived

For each recipe, I tried to take into consideration possible trade routes, time period, culture, climate, and a number of other factors. When I occasionally break with those rules, I make a note of it in the recipes, i.e. adding lemon to fish in Hobbiton.

Works Consulted:
Cottage of Lost Play
The Hobbit
The Fellowship of the Ring
The Two Towers
Return of the King
Children of Hurin
Lost Tales
Letters of Tolkien

A full bibliography and list of citations is available online at
www.theshirecookbook.com/bibliography

Acknowledgments

Brent, as always, for his tireless encouragement and patience.

Kira Yeversky for her sketches of flora and fauna

Etsy artists:

- Erika Rae Heins (shop: ErikaRaeHeins) for her sketches of the fireside scene and stacked dishes.
- Claire McCann (shop: Nafftastic) for her artwork of the Shire in winter
- Chad Ensien (shop: coffeeandwatercolors) for the country scene watercolor
- Georgiana (shop: BluebellBumblebees) for the scans of flowers

About the Author

Chelsea grew up in rural New York, surrounded by cows and an appreciation for small farms. However, her real love affair with food began during a year abroad in Turkey, which sparked a passion for both culinary matters and history. A lifelong artist and fantasy fan, she greatly enjoys foreign languages, treasure hunting, and all things related to honey. Like the literature she loves, Chelsea's work is a synthesis of imagination and historical research. She is focused on bringing other fantasy worlds to life through food, photography, art, and digital media. She and her husband live in an old Vermont farmhouse with a retired hound and one very plump Manx cat.

Made in the USA
San Bernardino, CA
20 March 2017